Soul Garden

WHY YOU ARE HUMAN ON EARTH

LINDSAY MANN

HARTSDALE, NY

Dedicated to my teachers.

INTRODUCTION

If you are reading this, you likely reflect on the mysteries of your existence, such as who you are, why you exist, and your purpose. You may have beliefs and theories about it, but no one seems to have the answers, so your curiosity is left to wonder.

Sometimes, believing that there is meaning in everything can be deeply fulfilling, while other times, it can be liberating to think that nothing matters at all. Whatever you choose, you can always tell when experiences have a tremendous impact on your life. You feel it in your Soul.

What is a Soul? What does it look like? Is it something that surrounds you? Is it centered inside of you? As a medium, I've gathered from my spiritual connections that it's like a wisp of energy consciousness or a clear, smoky S-shape in the air. I imagine that this wisp of energy drops in and out of living forms as it lives and dies and then floats around, existing in consciousness until it slips into its next life. But who knows?

What do you believe about the nature of the Soul? And do you think you only live once, or do you believe your Soul never dies? Does your Soul choose your lives, or is everything by chance? Is living on Earth a choice?

The beauty of life on Earth is truly miraculous. Still, the ongoing wars, violence, global mental health issues, and the devastating climate crisis can make it difficult to understand why you would choose to experience life in a world of such chaos and destruction.

When humanity perpetuates suffering and creates a living hell for ourselves, it can be hard to fathom this as a choice you continue to make. Despite the challenges, you are a resilient being who perseveres, adapts, and evolves because you believe life is a precious blessing.

You seek freedom, love, peace, happiness, well-being, prosperity, and a fully lived life. You crave meaningful bonds, belonging, adventure, empowerment, knowledge, and wisdom. You ride a collective rollercoaster amid all life's highs and lows. Why?

This book explores the concept of being a Soul living as a human on Earth today. It seeks guidance from the Akashic Records to understand our existence better, asking questions about the Soul's essence, its interconnections, growth, and the purpose of life on Earth. Whenever I grapple with life's perplexities, I find solace in the voice of this Universal information field. The Records always provide the clarity I need to keep moving forward, and I hope they do the same for you.

WHAT IS A SOUL?

A Soul is an eternal,
unique flow of energy,
ever-changing.

A Soul exists in the ether that moves and thrives among other Souls — bouncing, dancing, circling, holding, releasing, and existing within the parameters of an atmospheric ecosystem.

Souls share information, giving and receiving, keeping and burying, unearthing and letting go in cycles and loops of existence.

Souls are bound to one
another only as you let them
be, believing deeply in the
bond or not.

Belief systems, genetic makeups, traditions, education, and environments shape the shells of Souls. This is who you are, the character you get to play in each lifetime.

Souls remain and continue
to move through all lifetimes,
forming ideas, benefitting
the Soul's progression, and
sharing information with
other Souls, ultimately to
keep moving forward.

A Soul temporarily lives in
a form, knowing that this
form will come to completion
when it can no longer move
forward in that form.

Physical form eventually
breaks down because it
can only maintain its well-
being among the elements of
material existence
for so long.

Commonly, as humans,
you attach to your form,
cherishing its impact and
preciousness and fearing or
dreading its end.
However, you can return if
and when your Soul is willing
to try again.

Every interaction between Souls has a ripple effect: the more interactions, the more complex the effects. Short-term or long-term interactions do not measure the impact between Souls.

The force behind one Soul to another Soul is the measure of impact: the Consciousness, the willingness, the power of the intention of the Soul to make an impact.

Ideas of the Soul are limited only by your conditions, beliefs, and capacity to be willing to expand or not expand the experience of your Soul journey.

Physical restraints limit certain aspects of your Soul's abilities, but the mind can imprison it. Open your mind, expand your Soul. Possibilities are endless in the purpose of a Soul.

You are a choice. You chose
to be who you are in this
lifetime and every lifetime
before you, and you will
choose your lifetimes
in the future.

Free will to choose is your Soul's birthright in every lifetime. You innately have the freedom to choose.

Limits are only belief systems
and, sometimes, physical
restraints of your Soul's life
choosing.

A Soul is a never-ending,
unbreakable, consistent
rising and falling flow
of energy within an
ecosystem of countless other
flows of energy.

Tap into the rhythm of your Soul everywhere. You can always feel the flow of your Soul.

Like specks of dust, microorganisms, and the air you breathe, everything exists. Nothing does not exist. Coming in and out of consciousness of existence is one thing, but you and everything around you exist.

The fear, the vacuum, the void, the blackhole feeling of being sucked out of — or into — your body is the Universal knowing of the falsity of non-existence. This feeling can also be the transition from one form to the next.

To be non-existent is impossible. Consciousness, relatability, and awareness of interactions of any kind means to be in existence. The realization of something means that it exists.

Everything exists, whether
or not you are aware of it.
All spaces, everywhere, have
interactions of existence at
all times, in all forms.

Time, space, and the elements are part of existence — a constant, consistent, endless existence.

All existences exist at the same time. Everything happens all at once, all of the time, everywhere.

Souls are part of the flow of energy breaking off and forming into one, then breaking off again, coming and going, attaching and detaching.

You will always exist in this oversimplified form; this thread of you continues on and on and on.

Existing is an eternal
experience for everyone.
Moving and flowing among
each other at different times
in different spaces.

Jumping in and out of various forms of existence is a playful thing — a charming change of possibilities. Lives are short commitments in the timeline of eternity. Seemingly long or short, depending on your chosen life character.

Dissociating, or watching yourself from outside of your body, is your Soul jumping out to separate for a time to take a look at yourself, usually in a moment of existential crisis. This is a self-check-in of the Soul.

Souls are divine enthusiasts diving deep. You choose to change and experience the metamorphosis of life in various forms.

Life is being given a chance
to change through the depths
of forms, embracing and
releasing, contracting and
expanding inside and out.

WHAT ARE SOUL CONNECTIONS?

Soul connections are
the deepest levels of knowing
one another.

You've lived many lives together. You like finding each other to learn from each other. You attach by threads of similarities — past, present, and sometimes future.

You know and understand
your characters through the
facades of your forms.
You see through the eyes into
the consciousness, matter,
mannerisms,
energy, and flow of your
particular characters.
You *know* each other.

Souls reunite for lessons to learn, check-ins, and honest reflections for growth (or not). Fractions and facets, angles, changes, evolution (or not). You check in with each other for reflections on yourselves since the last meeting.

There is no judgment towards a Soul connection unless current character belief systems create judgment for the internal balance of the Soul's fears to quell the character's fears of the self.

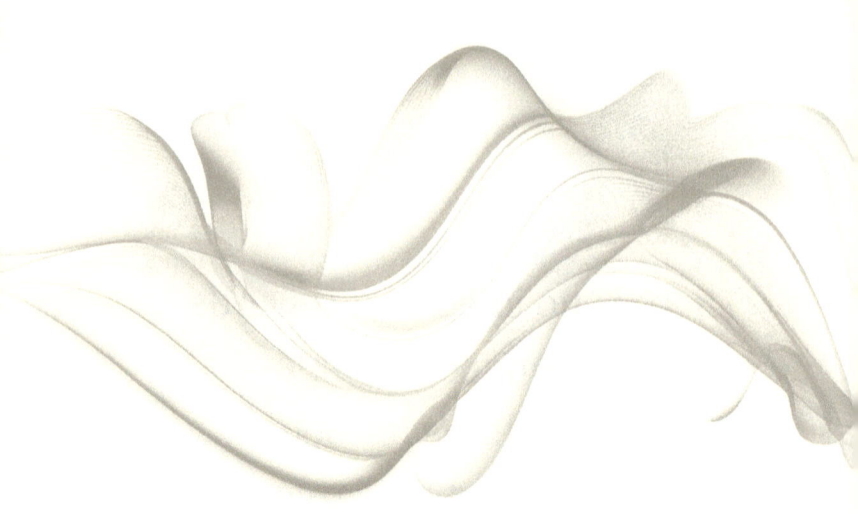

Reunions inspire self-examination, "Have I grown since we last met? Have I changed?" There are no failures, just check-ins. Characters create the belief system of failure and success, not the Soul.

Soul connections help to ground you into a deeper, more meaningful life through familiarity, commonality, and belonging. They ground you into your lifetimes as staples, benchmarks, timelines, and notches of impact.

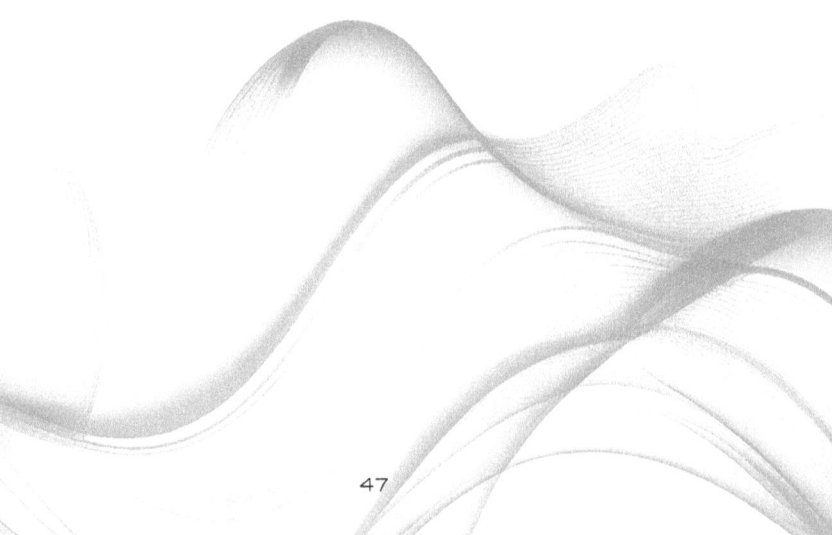

When you say, "I remember,"
you build memories
together—creating moments
and memorable experiences
of powerful flowing energy —
the creations and expressions
of your Soul's impact.

One Soul creates impact. Two Souls together generate more impact, and so on. The more Souls that combine in special impactful moments, the more expansive the collective experience of that special impactful moment becomes.

Souls come together for impact and have a limitless potential of possibilities together.

If you ever feel disconnected from your Soul, first acknowledge that you are a Soul and that your Soul is the foundation of your character. Second, see others as Souls, just like you.
Commit to the knowledge of your existence and the existence of others as Souls.

When you feel a Soul connection, celebrate finding each other. You spread far and wide, sometimes missing each other in entire lifetimes, but not forever. It's an immense gift to find your Soul connections.

If you don't believe in your Soul, you won't believe in the Souls of others, and you will struggle to find your Soul connections. That's okay. That's your journey in this lifetime.

There is no right or wrong
way to be a Soul. You just are.
Nothing needs to be done.

HOW DOES A SOUL GROW?

Souls grow through choice,
chance, and change.

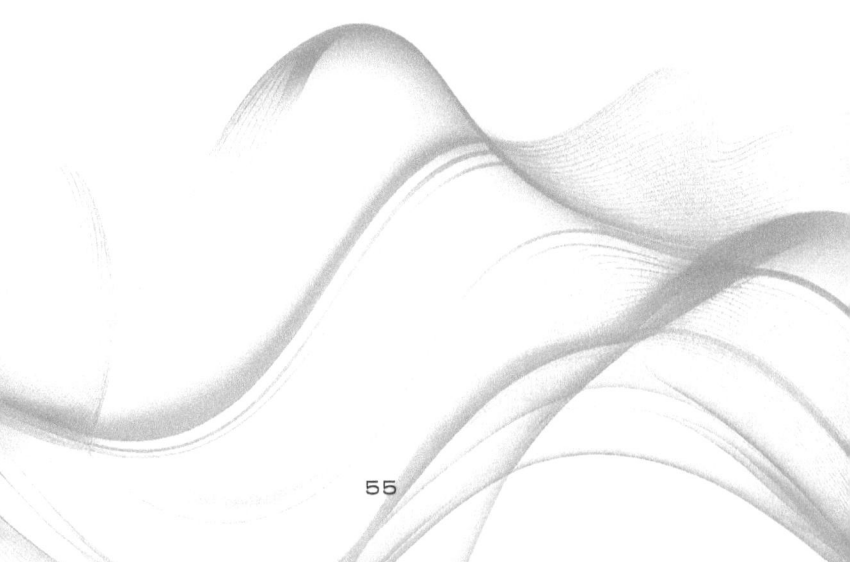

Soul growth is attained only through experiences and interactions. No movement? No growth. No interactions? No growth. No experiences? No growth.

Souls grow through
environmental changes,
sensations, emotions,
inspiration, failures, creation,
destruction, miracles,
impressions, expression, free
will, willpower, and all forces
of change.

Growth is unlimited and never-ending. All perceived endings are doors to new beginnings for growth.

The things that move you move your Soul. Don't underestimate the power of movement, however small. When you move, others move, too. They move with you, away from you, towards you, and in all directions.

Every movement has an impact. Butterflies to hurricanes. Whether gentle or forceful, solid or fluid, visible or invisible. All elements move — earth, air, fire, water, and ether.

A Soul grows through
experiences of movement,
pressure, force, and fluidity.
Even stagnancy grows.

By resisting movement,
you build strength against
the change pulling you. You
become stronger in your will
not to move. But the pull
will ultimately move you in
a direction. All must move
eventually.

Fluidity, surrender, and receptivity allow for the ease of movement to change and, thus, grow faster.

"How will this change me?" and "How will I grow?" are powerful questions for the Soul. Ask your Soul these questions, and your whole being will shift into its next growth phase.

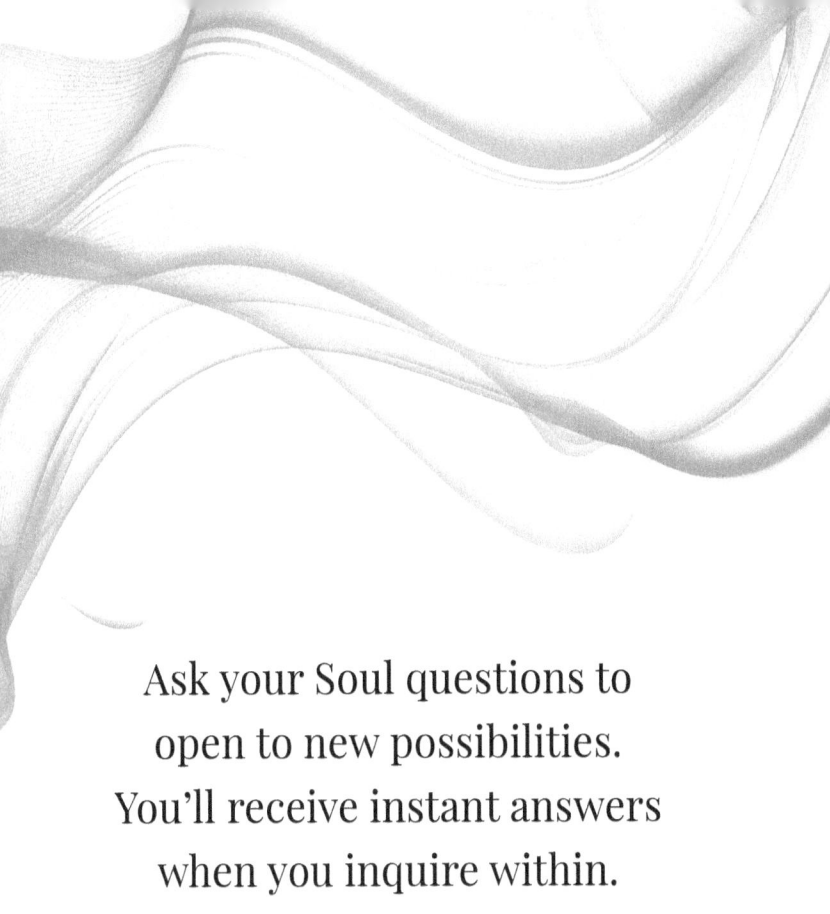

Ask your Soul questions to
open to new possibilities.
You'll receive instant answers
when you inquire within.

Through experiences
embedded in the imprint
of your being, your Soul
has opportunities to follow
through to the truth of your
existence in a lifetime.

Decisions create change. Chance creates pathways to more decisions to create more change. The outcome is almost always change, thus growing the Soul's experience.

Souls grow best through truth, trust, and the willingness and openness to change. Opening is growing into expansion and the fullness of being a Soul.

WHAT IS THE PURPOSE OF LIFE ON EARTH?

The purpose of life on
Earth is to be held in a body
encapsulated in existence.

Earth is a true and whole
experience of living in a life-
filled world.
All of life combined in
a place for a time.

An array of possibilities in
the surroundings thrive
and change simultaneously,
independently yet
interdependently, touching,
feeling, and sensing blasts
of encounters.

Life on Earth is a playful
existence if chosen for
that purpose — role-
playing games.

Earth is a place to be found, seen, and heard. To exist and create. To be part of everything, everywhere, all at once, in a large-scale, diverse ecosystem. A never-ending parade of life.

Earth is a Soul Garden — a complex and constantly changing accumulation of all life elements that consists of numerous layers and interactions between different lives, occurring for blips of time in space.

Earth is a wondrous,
ever-evolving, stunning,
moving landscape of
interconnections weaving
and affecting one another
at all times.

It is the external reflection of all the inner worlds of all life and vice versa. A constant reflection of life. Earth changes and forms, as do the lives on it.

The magnetic field of Earth inspires you to come back to it often. Its magnetism is enchanting. Its pulsing light, glow, and dark crevices for exploration create endless mysteries to solve.

Earth is abundantly fruitful,
feeding all life on it, specific
to each life form. There are
treasures to be discovered
underneath and above
the surfaces.
Growth is everywhere.

Earth is a heaven when you co-create and live in well-being among all living things. It is a flourishing, dynamic source of resources for growth — a garden for Souls.

You forever dive from the sky back into Earth to find a way to keep going forward, changing, moving, and exploring for your Soul's growth.

Earth's glowing ball of light and life is a promise of new experiences, guaranteed change, and evolution for your Soul.
You enter with great risk but promise for growth.

Earth is for exploration and adventure, witnessing changes over time on the planet and in the people. You like to experience what's happening now, then leave and come back in the future to see it again.

Souls push perceived
limitations through evolution.
Evolution is an education and
an experiment; what
has evolved, and what can
evolve more?

The movement, intensity, and portals opening and closing all the time, in all spaces, make it almost impossible not to want to come back to Earth to explore and experience all that happens here.

Earth is a choice of
aliveness. Few Souls desire
to experience lifelessness
because there is an inherent
need for movement and
growth through the changes
of being alive.

No matter what changes occur, they evolve the Soul. There is no good or bad change and no judgment in the catalysts for your evolutionary shifts.

Connection is the most
significant theme on
Earth now — how Souls
are connecting or not. All
experiences of connection
are available and pushing
boundaries.

The exploration
of connection and
disconnection is underlying
the evolution of all Souls on
Earth today.

Soul Garden, Earth, is the most sacred place in all time and space.

Honoring the full spectrum
of experiences *unattached*
defeats the point of choosing
to live here.

Get *ROCKED*.
It's why you chose to be here.
Experience, grow, change,
and be in the movement
of everything.

CONCLUSION

Right now, you have the gift of being alive. It's easy to become consumed by life's traumas and distracted by the chaos that keeps you from seeing the bigger picture. Nevertheless, you can shape your experiences and choose who you wish to become, what you desire to do here, and who you want to join you along the ride.

Knowing that it can be difficult to appreciate life sometimes, try to see it with new eyes as often as possible. Zoom out and tune out the noise to marvel at this extraordinary ecosystem you are part of. The ugly human stuff belongs to help you grow. It's the compost you need to make rich soil for your blossoming. Stop buying into the drama of doom and envision better for the planet that provides you with everything you need, in abundance and for free.

Earth is the place where your Soul comes to grow. As you close chapters of your life, carry the lessons that benefit you into your next adventure and leave the rest behind. Continue to play, learn, and evolve in this garden that your Soul returns to time and time again. While you're here, create the world you want to live in, not only for future generations but for you when you want to come back lifetimes into the future.

ABOUT THE AUTHOR

Lindsay Mann is an intuitive healing artist from New York who teaches spiritual and energetic support and guidance practices. Soul Garden is Lindsay's third self-published book. Her other books include *Beyond Love: A Collection of Channeled Messages from Passed-On Loved Ones* and *30 Questions to Ask the Akashic Records to Change the World*. Learn more about Lindsay and her work at www.heyclarity.com.